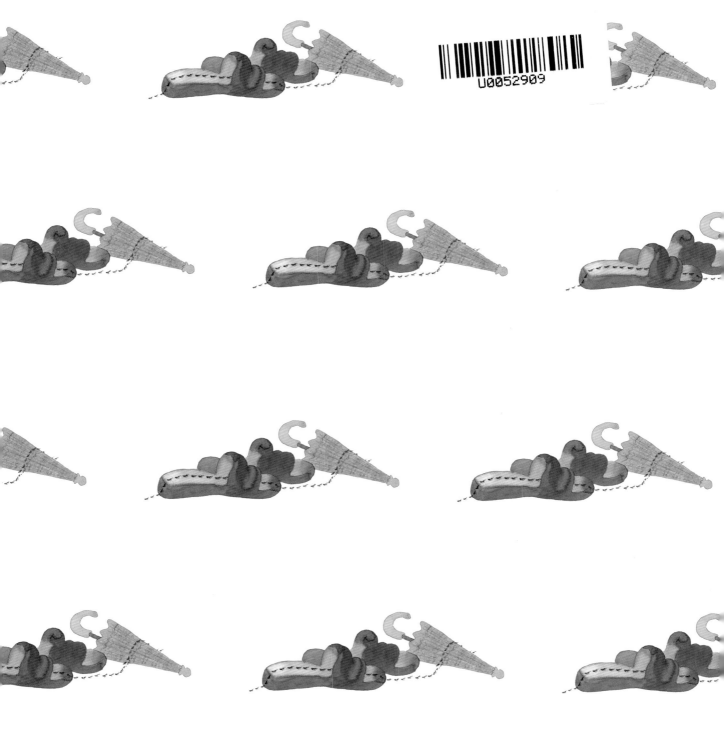

For Rigel

There Are Ants in My Pants!

唉呀！
褲子裡有螞蟻

Kathleen R. Seaton／著

姚　紅／繪

"Look!" said Grandmother.

"Ants!" cried Mother.

"A very long line of ants,"
said Father.

A very long train of ants came under the door and into our house.

"Where are they going?"
asked Little Brother.
"Into my *slippers," said Grandfather.
"And out again."

*為生字，請參照生字表

"Over and under my umbrella,"
Little Sister said.

"Inside and outside my book bag,"
said Big Brother.

6

"Between my homework,"
Big Sister said.

7

"Across the television," said Grandmother.

8

The ants *marched over the sofa and into the kitchen.

Over the table and down the chairs they went.

9

"What do they want?" I cried.

"Something to eat," said Grandfather.

"Something sweet," said Little Brother.

The ants marched on.

Then, up the *stairs they went, *step by step.

One by one they soon *disappeared.

13

"Where did they go?" Grandfather asked.

"I don't know," Grandmother *replied.

"Maybe they're *taking a nap."

14

Everyone sat down and waited.

It was so very quiet.

Soon, we heard a *thump! Thump! **Thump!**

Down the stairs they came with something very large.

"What's that?" *screamed Big Sister, climbing on a chair.

"What do they have?" *squeaked Little Sister,
standing on the sofa.

"EEEEK!" Grandmother cried,
holding Mother very *tightly.

17

Father went closer. "Pants!" Father *roared.

"They have a pair of pants!"

"Pants?" everyone cried.

I stood behind Father for a look.

"Oh!" I *yelled.

"The ants have my pants!"

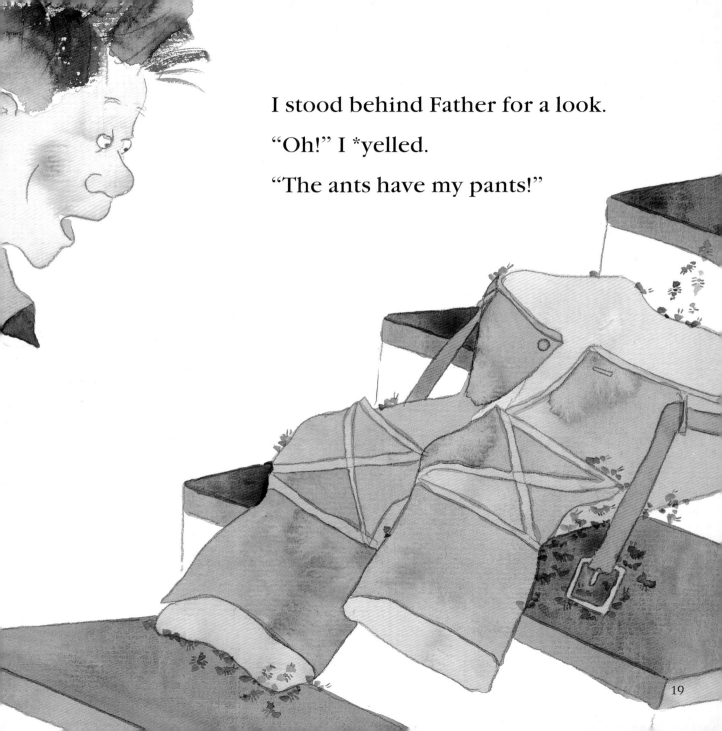

*Suddenly the ants stopped and my pants fell to the floor. Up the legs and down they went. Around and about the belt they danced. In and out of the *pockets they ran. This way and that they moved.

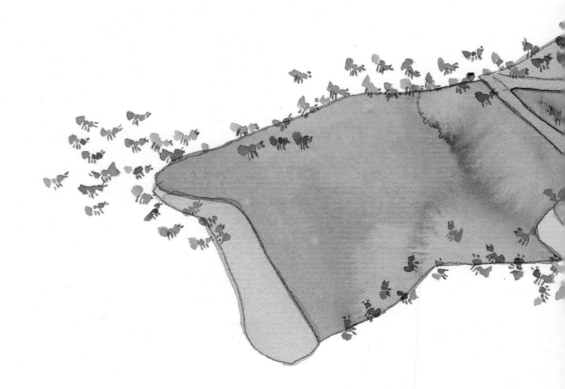

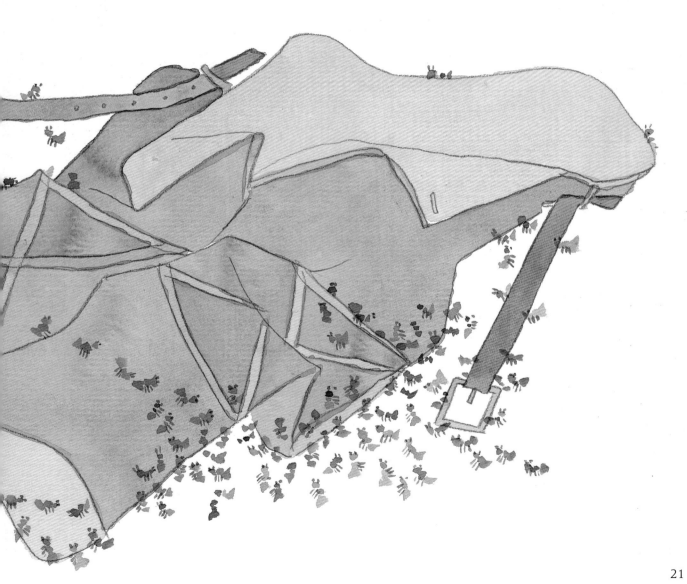

"Ants! Ants!" I screamed. "There are ants in my pants!"

Everyone just *stared. Very slowly all the ants went to one pocket.

"What are they doing?" Grandfather asked.

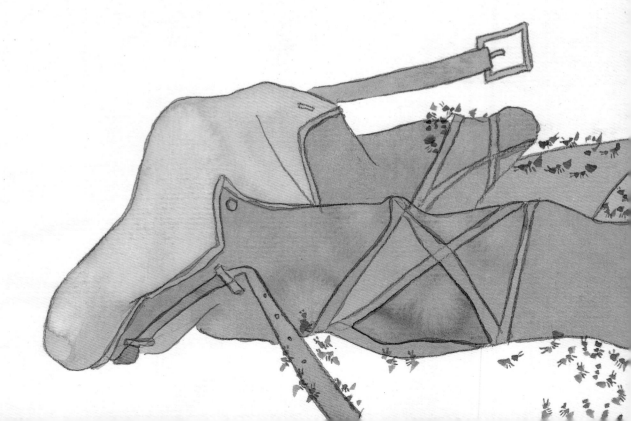

Before anyone could answer, out they came carrying a little pink candy. Across the floor and out the door they went, taking my candy with them.

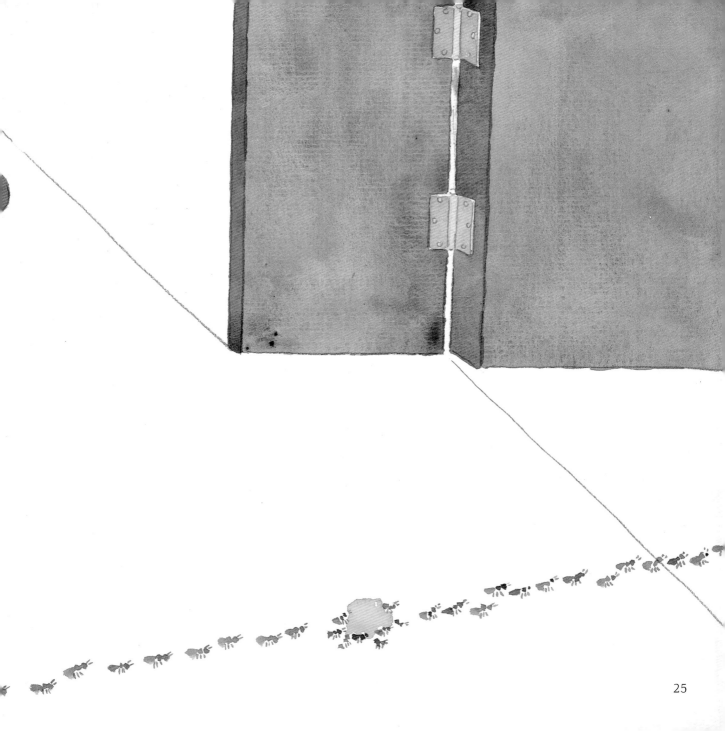

生ㄕㄥ 字ㄗˋ 表ㄅㄧㄠˇ

adv.= 副ㄈㄨˋ詞ㄘˊ， n.= 名ㄇㄧㄥˊ詞ㄘˊ， v.= 動ㄉㄨㄥˋ詞ㄘˊ

唉呀！褲子裡有螞蟻！

p.2-3

奶奶說：「你們看！」

媽媽大叫：「有螞蟻！」

爸爸說：「好長一排螞蟻啊！」

一條非常長的螞蟻隊伍從門底下走進我們的房子。

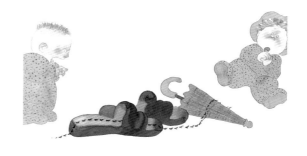

p.4-5

弟弟問：「他們要去哪裡啊？」

爺爺說：「他們走進我的拖鞋，又走出來了。」

妹妹說：「他們爬上我的傘，又爬到傘下面。」

p.6-7

哥哥說：「他們走進我的書包，又走出來了。」

姐姐說：「他們鑽進了我的作業簿。」

p.8-9

奶奶說：「他們橫越了電視機。」
螞蟻們齊步翻越了沙發，然後
走進廚房；爬上了桌子，又爬
到椅子下。

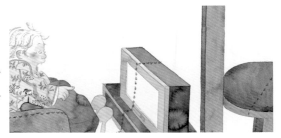

p.10-11

我叫著：「他們想做什麼？」
爺爺說：「找吃的東西吧！」
弟弟說：「找甜的東西吧！」

p.12-13

螞蟻們繼續前進，然後他們一
步一步的上了樓梯。
很快的，他們一個接著一個消
失了。

p.14-15

爺爺說：「他們去哪裡了？」
奶奶回答：「我不知道，也許他們在睡午覺吧！」
大家都坐下來等。四周變得好安靜。

p.16-17

很快的，我們聽到了「砰！砰！砰！」的聲音。
螞蟻們爬下樓來，帶了一樣很大的東西。
姊姊爬上椅子，尖叫著說：「那是什麼？」
妹妹站在沙發上尖聲說：「他們拿了什麼？」
奶奶緊抓著媽媽大叫：「唉呀！」

p.18-19

爸爸走近點兒看。他大喊:「是褲子!他們拿了一條褲子!」

大家大叫:「褲子?」

我站到爸爸身後瞧了瞧。我大喊:「喔!螞蟻拿了我的褲子!」

p.20-21

螞蟻們突然停了下來,跟著,我的褲子掉到了地上。他們在褲腿上上下下的爬,又在皮帶附近跳起舞來。他們從口袋跑進跑出,又一下這邊一下那邊的移動著。

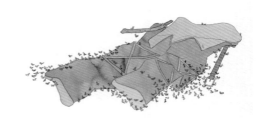

p.22-23

我尖叫著:「螞蟻啊!有螞蟻在我的褲子裡啊!」

大家就只是盯著瞧。螞蟻們非常緩慢的走進一個口袋。

爺爺問:「他們在做什麼啊?」

p.24-25

在還沒有人能回答之前，螞蟻們帶著一小塊粉紅色的糖果走了出來。然後，他們就帶著我的糖果，一路穿越地板，走出大門。

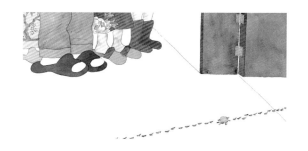

英文練習

　　哇！小班家裡怎麼有這麼多螞蟻跑進來呀？螞蟻們上上下下、前後左右的鑽來鑽去，也因此，故事裡用了好多形容「位置」的「介系詞」，把螞蟻們的動作描述得栩栩如生呢！讓我們來認識這些常用的「介系詞」吧！

① 認識介系詞
請聽 CD 的 Track 4，跟著一起唸下面六個介系詞。

under	inside	outside
在……下面	在……裡面	在……外面
between	across	into
在……之間	越過……	到……裡面

② 看图填单字

請按照圖片提示，將適當的介系詞填入空格中。
這些句子都可以在故事裡找到喔！

例 The cat is **under** the table.

1. The ants came u_____r the door.

2. The ants are going i____o my slippers.

3. The ants are b_____n my homework.

4. The ants are going a_____s the television.

5. The ants are o____e my book bag.

正確答案在第 31 頁喔！

認識螞蟻

　　大家好，我是小螞蟻安安，我和同伴們正要把小班牛仔褲口袋裡的糖果，搬回家去給女王陛下。什麼？你問我女王陛下是誰？她就是你們人類所說的蟻后啊！整個螞蟻王國都是由她統治。因為她背負著繁殖後代的重責大任，所以其他工作都交給我們這些小螞蟻們。例如我們工蟻，就負責尋找食物、建築蟻巢、照顧蟻后跟幼蟻；而強壯的兵蟻，就負責保護整個蟻巢的安全。常常聽人類誇獎我們是「小蟻雄兵」，其實，我們工蟻和兵蟻都是雌性的，所以應該是小蟻「雌」兵才對！當然囉，我們王國裡也有雄蟻，不過數量不多，主要任務也是繁殖後代，其他什麼事都不用做；因此我們螞蟻王國裡的大小事，可以說都是由女性當家作主喔！

　　嗯？你問我們怎麼發現小班牛仔褲口袋裡的糖果呀？這全靠我們頭上這一對敏銳的觸角喔！只要觸角一偵測到周圍有食物的存在，我們工蟻就會出發去尋找食物。別看我們個子小，我們可是大力士，能夠舉起比自己重上20倍的食物喔！而且在尋找食物的路上，我們還會釋放出一種叫「費洛蒙」的化學物質，其他的同伴會藉著「費洛蒙」獨特的氣味，一路找到我們，然後大家一起通力合作，把食物搬回家。這也是為什麼我們螞蟻都會整齊的排成一直線走，走再遠也不怕迷路的原因。哎呀！時間不早了，我和同伴們得快點把糖果搬回家才行，下次再聊囉，再見！

Kathleen R. Seaton is an Associate Professor in the Department of Foreign Languages and Literature at Tunghai University. She teaches a seminar course in Children's Literature, Film and Culture, courses in composition and oral practice and electives in acting and drama. She holds an interdisciplinary PhD in Mass Communication and an MFA in Film from Ohio University, Athens Ohio, U.S.A.

Kathleen R. Seaton （呂珍妮） 在東海大學外國語文學系擔任副教授。她教授兒童文學、電影與文化的文學討論課程，另外還開設英文作文和口語訓練兩堂主修課程，選修課程方面則有表演與戲劇。她擁有美國俄亥俄大學的大眾傳播學跨領域博士和電影藝術碩士學位。

寫書的人

　　姚紅畢業於南京藝術學院中國畫系，現職於江蘇少年兒童出版社，從事兒童繪本的編輯和創作多年。她的繪畫作品《蓬蓬頭溜冰的故事》獲第四屆中國優秀少年讀物一等獎；《牙印兒》獲國際兒童讀物聯盟「小松樹」獎；《飛吻大王》獲第五屆國家圖書獎。由姚紅策劃並與他人合作編輯的《「我真棒」幼兒成長圖畫書》獲 2000 年冰心兒童圖書獎。

畫畫的人

I Love My Family Series

我愛我的家 系列

Kathleen R. Seaton 著／姚紅 繪

附中英雙語朗讀 CD ／ 適讀對象：學習英文 0～2 年者（國小 1～3 年級適讀）

六本全新創作的中英雙語繪本，
六個溫馨幽默的故事，
帶領小朋友們進入單純可愛的小班的生活，
跟他一起分享和家人之間親密的感情！

Grandmother

Grandfather

Father

Mother

1. **I'm Bored** 我好無聊喔！　　　　國立台中教育大學英語教學系副教授

2. **Wake Up! Wake Up!** 起床了！　　　　　　　楊式美

3. **Let's Go! Let's Go!** 出發嘍！

4. **Happy Birthday Grandmother** 奶奶，生日快樂！

5. **I Want A Dog** 我想要一隻狗！

6. **There Are Ants in My Pants!** 哎呀！褲子裡有螞蟻

賽皮與柔依系列

ZIPPY AND ZOE SERIES

想知道我們發生了什麼驚奇又爆笑的事嗎？
歡迎學習英文0-2年的小朋友一起來分享我們的故事——
「賽皮與柔依系列」，讓你在一連串有趣的事情中學英文！

精裝／附中英雙語朗讀CD／全套六本

Carla Golembe 著／繪
本局編輯部 譯

Hello！我是賽皮，我喜歡畫畫、做餅乾，還有跟柔依一起去海邊玩。偷偷告訴你們一個秘密：我在馬戲團表演過喔！

Hi，我是柔依，今年最開心的事，就是賽皮送我一張他親手畫的生日卡片！賽皮是我最要好的朋友，他很聰明也很可愛，我們兩個常常一起出去玩！

賽皮與柔依系列有：

❶ 賽皮與綠色顏料
   (Zippy and the Green Paint)
❷ 賽皮與馬戲團
   (Zippy and the Circus)
❸ 賽皮與超級大餅乾
   (Zippy and the Very Big Cookie)
❹ 賽皮做運動
   (Zippy Chooses a Sport)
❺ 賽皮學認字
   (Zippy Reads)
❻ 賽皮與柔依去海邊
   (Zippy and Zoe Go to the Beach)

國家圖書館出版品預行編目資料

There Are Ants in My Pants!:唉呀!褲子裡有螞蟻 /
Kathleen R. Seaton著;姚紅繪;本局編輯部譯.－
－初版一刷.－－臺北市：三民，2006
　　面；　　公分.－－(Fun心讀雙語叢書.我愛我的
　　家系列)
中英對照
ISBN 957－14－4425－1　　(精裝)

1.英國語言－讀本

523.38　　　　　　　　　　　　　　94026448

網路書店位址　　http://www.sanmin.com.tw

© There Are Ants in My Pants!
——唉呀！褲子裡有螞蟻

著作人	Kathleen R. Seaton
繪　者	姚　紅
譯　者	本局編輯部
發行人	劉振強
著作財產權人	三民書局股份有限公司 臺北市復興北路386號
發行所	三民書局股份有限公司 地址／臺北市復興北路386號 電話／(02)25006600 郵撥／0009998－5
印刷所	三民書局股份有限公司
門市部	復北店／臺北市復興北路386號 重南店／臺北市重慶南路一段61號
初版一刷	2006年1月
編　號	S 806081
定　價	新臺幣壹佰捌拾元整

行政院新聞局登記證局版臺業字第○二○○號

ISBN　957－14－4425－1　　(精裝)